BASS BUILDERS

jump 'n' blues bass

by Keith Rosiér

Table of Contents

PLAYBACK+
Speed • Pitch • Balance • Loop

To access audio visit:
www.halleonard.com/mylibrary

Enter Code
2941-2048-6524-3412

ISBN: 978-0-7935-9166-4

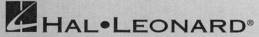

Visit Hal Leonard Online at
www.halleonard.com

Contact Us:
Hal Leonard
7777 West Bluemound Road
Milwaukee, WI 53213
Email: info@halleonard.com

In Europe contact:
Hal Leonard Europe Limited
Distribution Centre, Newmarket Road
Bury St Edmunds, Suffolk, IP33 3YB
Email: info@halleonardeurope.com

In Australia contact:
Hal Leonard Australia Pty. Ltd.
4 Lentara Court
Cheltenham, Victoria, 3192 Australia
Email: info@halleonard.com.au

Foreword

When I first met Keith Rosiér before a blues show on Catalina Island, he was wearing Bermuda shorts and a fedora, puffing on a big old stinky stogie, and tuning up a hollowbodied, cowhide-covered Ferrington bass that was strung with the fattest tapewounds I'd ever seen. At that time, I thought, "This guy is either a true blues dog or a total nut. Or maybe both." Fortunately, the latter was correct.

Keith can lay down a greasy blues groove that's so simple and soulful that you don't realize the finesse and the knowledge that went into making it. He's a blues bass scholar, for sure, but Keith also practices what he teaches. He knows you'll never get deep into blues unless you study the history, but he also knows that sometimes—most of the time—you just have to grab your ax and play. That's why this invaluable volume includes words you can read and music you can actually hear. Think of *Jump 'n' Blues Bass* as your own personal blues bass encyclopedia and instant jam session. Then pick up your bass, and lay down a groove. The hat and cigar are optional.

Richard Johnston
Editor, *Bass Player* magazine

Introduction

Learning to play authentic blues bass is the dream of many of today's bassists. Most players start out by listening to vintage blues recordings, hopefully learning and absorbing the style and the bass lines and applying them to their instrument. *Jump 'n' Blues Bass* has done the homework for you—providing real, vintage-style jump/swing bass lines in the style of legendary blues bassists like Willie Dixon, Larry Taylor (Hollywood Fats), and Edgar Willis (Ray Charles), as well as modern blues bass lines in the style of such contemporary players as Duck Dunn, Tommy Shannon (Stevie Ray Vaughan), and Keith Ferguson (the Fabulous Thunderbirds).

Along with playing lines in the style of famous blues bassists, you will also learn the necessary survival skills required of any working bassist. An easy-to-understand primer section shows you how to read bass clef if you are just getting started. (All of the subsequent examples include TAB.) There are also sections on grooving, practicing, time-keeping, how to get a good blues tone, what gear to use when recording, and how to set up an electric or an upright bass. A special section entitled "More Blues Bass Lines" provides you with a comprehensive study of the most popular bass lines in the blues repertoire. While you are having fun playing these classic lines with the live band on the accompanying audio tracks, you will be adding them to your own arsenal—making you a more knowledgeable and versatile blues bassist.

Jump 'n' Blues Bass is intended to be a valuable handbook for any bassist, whatever style or level. Beginners can learn authentic blues bass lines without having to purchase and transcribe numerous recordings; more advanced players can benefit from the survival skills and insights into bass playing that I've picked up from my own long experience in the music business. Whatever your current playing level, I hope you will be inspired to listen to early blues recordings while using these examples to help you further develop your own style. Finally, I would like to dedicate *Jump 'n' Blues Bass* to the late Edgar Willis, and the late Keith Ferguson, two of my all-time favorite bassists.

Now, pick up your bass, put on your shades, and start grooving!

Keith Rosiér

Keith Rosiér

Primer

Next to each musical example, you will see a black diamond; the number in the diamond corresponds to the track number. For example, **1** is the tuning track. Make sure that you check your own tuning against this track before starting.

1 **Tuning: G, D, A, E (high to low)**

If you wish to hear more of the backup band when playing along with the tracks, pan your stereo's balance control to the right. To hear more of the bass, pan to the left. All of the music is suitable for either acoustic or electric bass—so practice both!

If you're inexperienced in reading music, the following exercise should help get you started. Play along with the audio to make sure that you're reading the pitches and rhythms correctly.

2 Notes

The Groove

The word "groove" is the most important word in any musician's vocabulary. The ability to groove can sometimes be more important than what notes are actually played. For example, there are situations where the simple, uneducated, but strong groove-playing bassist will be chosen over the more trained, schooled bass player. Why? Because the ability to groove speaks volumes over the ability to play a bunch of notes real fast or accurately, particularly in a band setting.

What exactly is a groove? In the simplest terms, it is a style of playing that expresses rhythm with a consistent, hypnotic beat. The best way to tell if you are playing in the groove is to watch your audience—if they are dancing or tapping their feet, then you are in a groove. At the same time, the feel is also important. The way you make transitions from note to note is when your feel comes into play. For example, are you chopping off notes too quickly? Do you make transitions smoothly with a consistent attack for each note? Do you allow each note to blossom and realize its full rhythmic value before going on to the next note? These essential techniques are the common thread that connects professional bass players. In order to be an in-demand bassist, you need to be aware of all your notes and be willing to play in balance with the rest of the band.

To help you achieve a solid groove and good feel, try to keep the following in mind when playing your bass:

- *Play each note with a firm and consistent stroke.* This helps create a round, fat tone. Don't play lightly—turn your amp down instead. A strong groove requires a firm approach at all times.

- *Pay attention to note length*, and be sure that you don't stop your notes too quickly—longer tones work best in most situations. I also recommend recording yourself whenever possible in order to check on proper note length. Inexperienced players tend to cut off their notes too quickly, creating a rushed, thin groove. Allow each note to ring with its full value before going on to the next. Sometimes, when playing certain feels, a shorter note length approach might be called for,

but even then, be sure to stop the notes smoothly. This is very important advice. I recommend that you pay close attention to every note you play—your favorite bassist does, too.

- *Don't rush!* A bassist who plays on top of the beat or rushes will not find much work and will have a hard time grooving with other players. At the same time, don't think that playing behind the beat or dragging is grooving either. Rushing and dragging are both problems that occur when a player does not have good time-keeping skills. Paying attention at all times will help you be aware of any time fluctuations. Use your ears, and develop your self-awareness when playing—this will help you become a better time-keeper.

- Play right *with* the drummer. Your bass and the drummer's kick drum should sound like they are being played by the same person. Playing tightly with the drummer will give a solid, grooving feel to the music. Make it a point not to fight rhythmically with the drummers that you work with—it only makes the band sound disjointed. Concentrate on adapting to each drummer's groove. By doing this, you will become very popular with drummers, and they will refer you for gigs because they know that you are easy to work with and a team player.

- Play *bass*. Too many bassists fall into the trap of playing too *much* or playing lines that are not appropriate for the bass or the song. The finest compliment that you can receive is that you play bass like a *bass player*, not like a frustrated guitarist. It is very important that you play solid, supportive lines that will complement the singer, song, and groove. This does not mean that you should play too simply; play the *right* bass line for the song, one that is neither too simple nor too busy.

Learn to listen to yourself, and quickly adjust your part if you feel that it is not working. Remember: Bass players who play too busily will not be as popular as solid supportive bassists.

Practicing

No matter how accomplished you become as a player, you will always need to practice. A consistent practice schedule is very important, especially if you don't work much with your band. Think of your musical ability as a muscle; it can't be maintained, much less developed, without playing and exercise.

The late Jaco Pastorius practiced scales and used them as the basis for his approach. Considering that all music is based on scales, knowledge of them is important to any serious bassist. Memorize the following major scale exercises, so that you can play them in any key or position. For instance, for the first exercise, start

on the low E note, and play the exercise in the key of E major. Then play the exercise in F major. Continue to play the exercise, moving up a half step at a time on the low E string, until you reach the twelfth fret. *Use this scale exercise for your daily warm-up.* Play the second exercise in all twelve major keys as well. Through repetition, you will develop a better ear and the ability to locate notes on the fingerboard when playing unfamiliar phrases. You will also become comfortable playing in all positions on the neck. *Always practice with a metronome!*

3 E Major Scale

G Major Scale in Thirds

It's also useful to know the difference between major and minor. If you don't, you will make mistakes like playing a major third in a minor key—most of you know what this sounds like. For example, in the key of G major, the third note of the scale is B-natural; in G minor, the third note is B-flat. A minor third is the same as a *flatted* major third. Just remember the following:

- In major keys, the I, IV, and V chords are all *major*; the rest of the chords are minor. The exception to this is the vii° chord, which is diminished (a.k.a., "minor 7 flat 5").

- In minor keys, the i, iv, and v chords are all *minor*; the rest of the chords are major. The exception in this case is the ii° chord, which is diminished (or "minor 7 flat 5").

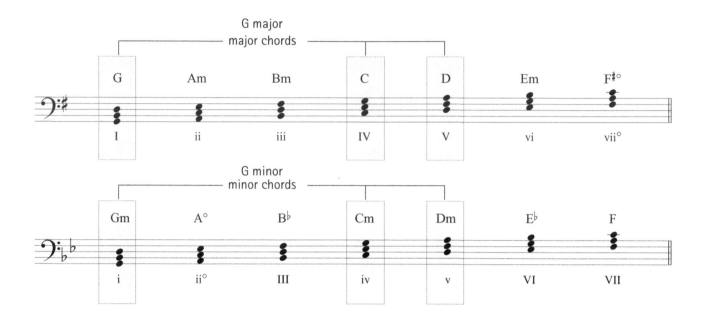

Artist's Spotlight
L a r r y   T a y l o r

If you say "West Coast jump blues," to most people, the name Larry Taylor immediately springs to mind. Larry is a respected upright and electric bassist who lives in Los Angeles, California. His credits include Hollywood Fats, Junior Watson, Kim Wilson, Al Blake, Philip Walker, Lynwood Slim, and Tom Waits.

Well-versed and knowledgeable in the blues tradition, Larry's bass lines have a classic, "retro" vibe to them, and he is a master of jump/swing bass playing. He also uses the "two-five" figure (a.k.a., "two-five substitution") very effectively, which is one of the aspects of his style that we will be studying. For example, in the following piece, the ii ("two") chord walking up to the V ("five") is played by the bass, while the rest of the band sits on the V chord. This figure is often used as a substitute for the traditional V-IV change at the end of a 12-bar blues before the turnaround.

As a session bassist, Larry has the ability to duplicate classic recorded bass sounds with his upright and Kay-brand hollowbody electric bass guitar. The "tone generator" for his upright bass sound is his carved German bass, strung with La Bella gut strings (Pro Set #980—metalwound gut E and A, with plain gut G and D) and played through a Rick Turner pickup system (Rick Turner Guitars, Los Angeles, CA).

Like other great blues/jump bassists, Larry occasionally throws in some nice rockabilly "slapping," and he can really swing. His popularity can also be attributed to his rock-solid time, appropriate note choices, and "never-too-busy" playing approach. When I first started playing blues in L.A., a blues guitarist gave me some recordings that Larry had played on and told me to "shed" ("woodshed") his lines. I did, and now you can too; here are some killer lines in the style of blues great Larry Taylor.

In the style of LARRY TAYLOR

The Metronome

What does a metronome have to do with grooving and blues bass playing? A lot, actually. When you don't have a good drummer or band to work with, you need someone or something to play with. After all, playing music is about interacting with people and having fun, and you must constantly adjust to each other in order to make it sound good. If you spend all your time playing by yourself, without a drummer, metronome, or drum machine, you will find it hard to interact with other players because you will be used to "plowing your own row," so to speak.

It is crucial that you be able to blend in and create music with other musicians, because if you are not flexible and willing to bend, you will never be a popular bassist; people will not be able to create freely when playing with you.

If you spend time playing with a metronome or drum machine, you will become aware of any tendencies that you have such as speeding up or slowing down. A strong sense of time is essential to the working bassist, and this, along with your ability to play a strong groove, will put you in demand. Time-keeping and grooving go hand in hand, and the bassists featured in this book all display a strong groove/time sense in their playing.

If you have trouble playing with a metronome, then you have problems with your time. If this is the case, you will probably have trouble playing with others, too. Good time-keeping skills can be developed with a little patience. Below are a few good exercises that will strengthen your time:

- Have the metronome count two beats per measure instead of four. For example, if you would normally play with the metronome set at 80 bpm (beats per minute), set it at 40 bpm instead. Then play along, counting four beats per measure, with the metronome beating only on beats 2 and 4 of each measure—this simulates the backbeat of a drummer.

- Practice all your grooves with a metronome at different tempos. This will develop your ability to play at different tempos comfortably. If you practice at the same tempo all the time, you will tend to drift to that tempo when playing your bass.

- Practice slow tempos, concentrating on note length. Most bassists have trouble playing very slow tempos smoothly. Remember: each note has a definite beginning and ending, so pay attention to every note.

- Play major and minor scales up and down the neck and across the strings, connecting each note. This will improve your ear and help your shuffle feels.

Artist's Spotlight
Willie Dixon

The late, legendary Willie Dixon was the undisputed king of blues and roots bass. As an upright bassist with many skills—including slapping, strong walking lines, and roots rock 'n' roll playing—Willie was an in-demand session bassist for countless major blues and rock artists. His list of clients was long and varied and included Little Walter, Willie Mabon, Muddy Waters, Howlin' Wolf, Bo Diddley, Lowell Fulson, Chuck Berry, and many others.

The West Coast "jump" style was directly influenced by Willie, as were the stylings of many of today's "roots rockers" and traditional blues bassists. You might wonder how a single bassist/songwriter could influence so many genres in the span of forty years, but consider the great number of recordings that Willie played on or wrote that are considered classics. His influence has been felt overseas and throughout the world of music.

Not necessarily a technical virtuoso, Willie's strengths were his abilities to groove and to communicate emotion through his music, both as an artist and a sideman. He also had a knack for making even the simplest bass lines work—never seeming "pedestrian" or inappropriate—proving that bass in its simplest form is a strong, valid means of expression.

Willie's bass playing was very unique. Using a gut-string bass, he fashioned an out-of-the-ordinary approach that included slaps, varied counterpoint rhythms, and jaw-droppingly fast runs. I highly recommend that you purchase the early recordings of Chuck Berry, as well as the *Willie Dixon* box set available from Chess/MCA Records. The Chess box set allows you to hear the great Willie Dixon in many different musical settings. Enjoy.

In the style of WILLIE DIXON

14

 # Getting a Good Blues Tone

Electric Bass

A set of flatwound strings is a good starting point. Flatwound strings work well because of the decreased treble response and strong fundamental note (bottom). The round "thuddy" tone produced by these strings is desirable when playing traditional blues and jump.

The shorter note duration of some flatwounds can sometimes work to your advantage—great for up-tempo walking lines and "funky" blues tunes. For most instruments, 45–105 gauge works best and is a good all-around tension. Some players like a heavier 50–110 gauge set—it depends on your hand strength and string action.

Nylon tapewound flatwound strings are another type of string that can work well for blues gigs. They sound deep and "throbby," with an upright-like tone. These strings also sound great on acoustic and semi-acoustic basses like Kramer-Ferrington, Kay, and Washburn. La Bella makes a good tape set (760N) available from Carvin. A product called Joha string oil makes playing on tapewounds and flatwounds much smoother and easier on the hands.

If you are playing in a modern-style blues band, a roundwound set can give you a little more fidelity and treble. Be careful though, because the hi-fi, trebly tone can sometimes work against you on blues jobs. I'll give you an example. I was called for a session and wasn't told what type of music I would be playing. Not expecting a blues session, I brought a Fender Jazz Bass with EMG pickups and a new set of roundwound strings on the bass. The engineer complained about my "too clean" bass tone and felt it wasn't right for the tune. I was going direct, so I was "married" to the tone of the bass and strings. The problem was not the Jazz Bass, though—it was the bright, ringing tone of the strings. This is not to say that new roundwounds are not good strings; they were simply the wrong string choice for that particular session. The moral of the story is this: keep a set of flatwounds on hand so that you can put them on your bass if needed. If you never change the strings on your bass, then you probably won't have to worry about getting a funky tone.

TIP

Once a new string is brought up to pitch, it should never be loosened below or tightened past the tuning point that it was designed for. If a string has been detuned or overtightened, it will never sound as good or be as "true" as it is when new and properly tuned. Also, never boil your strings; it makes them sound "flabby." Replace worn strings with a new set.

Upright Bass

Gut strings sound great, but dealing with the inherent problems associated with them is something to consider. Gut stretches and shrinks with temperature fluctuations, sometimes causing tuning problems. Gut strings can also be rough on the fingers (blisters). Amplifying a bass with gut strings is hard to do, especially when working with loud bands. La Bella's Pro Set #980 metalwound gut strings work well and last longer than plain gut, but like most manufacturers, they don't make metalwound G and D strings—only E and A. Pirastro String Co. makes sets (Olive and Eudoxa) of metalwound E, A, D, and G, but they do not recommend them for "slapping" because they will unravel. La Bella also makes a set of gut strings with nylon outer-winding that might work for you if the feel of plain gut, with its sometimes "nicked-up" outer wrap, bothers you. When using gut sets, applying Joha string oil will improve the feel and life of plain and wound strings.

To apply Joha oil:

1. Loosen the strings slightly. *(Do not loosen the strings more than one turn of your tuner—if there is not enough pressure from the strings on the top of the bass, the soundpost will fall over!)*

2. Take a fine emery cloth (new) and gently go over the entire length of the string, smoothing out any rough spots.

3. Saturate a small section (the size of a nickel) of a clean rag with Joha oil, and apply the oil over the entire length of the string.

Metal strings are widely used, with Thomastik Spiro-Core being the most popular. They are available in Orchestra and Solo tunings. (Orchestra is standard tuning; Solo is tuned up a step—F#, B, E, and A, low to high) The Orchestra tuning is what everyone uses, and it is available in two gauges: Orchestra mittel (medium gauge) and Orchestra weich (light gauge). Orchestra mittel can be a little heavy for some players. Weich gauge is very popular with its easy tension. I would recommend "weich" over "mittel" unless you have good hand strength. Playing four sets a night can wear down your strength, so start with a lighter tension.

For a gut-sounding steel string, try a set of Jargar medium gauge. These strings are not as trebly-sounding as Spriro-Cores and will be a good compromise for bassists preferring a gut string sound—without the disadvantages.

Incidentally, the G and D strings of most metal strings do tend to have more pronounced treble response than the E and A strings. Some players are not bothered by this, but many are. With most metal sets, when playing on the E and A strings, the sound is generally rounder and deeper, but when making the transition from low strings to high, the greater treble response of the G and D strings can sometimes be undesirable. To compensate for this, some bassists have tried using Jargar medium-gauge for the G and D only, with Spiro-Core weich or La Bella 7720 medium-gauge for the E and A strings, but the Jargar strings don't have as much sustain as a metal spiral or rope-core string. Some players use all-metal steel for the E and A strings with gut for the D and G, but the tension and tone difference of gut and metal might be too great on some basses.

Below are some custom string sets used by pro players:

- Thomastik Spiro-Core metal weich-gauge E and A strings with La Bella plain gut G and D strings
- Thomastik Spiro-Core metal Orchestra-gauge E and A strings with weich-gauge D and G strings
- Thomastik Spiro-Core metal weich E and A strings with Pirastro "Jazzer" G and D strings
- La Bella Pro Set #980 metalwound gut E and A strings with plain gut D and G strings

- La Bella Pro Set #7720 metal medium-gauge rope core
- La Bella #7710 metal with nylon tapewound set (heavier gauge than #7720)
- La Bella Goldentone Set #4000—all strings nylon-wound on gut
- Jargar medium-gauge—metal strings that sound like gut (short decay)

PURCHASE ORCHESTRA TUNING SETS ONLY!

If you are getting blisters from your metal strings, try putting a little bit of Joha oil on your metal strings, then lightly wipe off the excess. I use Joha oil on my steel strings at the beginning of every set—it makes them very easy to play. (Also, by the end of the set it has usually evaporated, which is very convenient.) Some upright bassists put a small amount of Vaseline behind their ear, occasionally touching that spot for lubrication, thus keeping their plucking fingers soft and slick. Try Finger-Ease spray, too.

When playing long hours on the upright, the pinky finger and the first finger of the fretting hand get the most wear and tear because of the sliding and shifting. On the plucking hand, the first finger can become fatigued and sore. This is a problem for all upright players, and lubrication can lessen the blistering.

A great product that eliminates blisters is called Elasto-Plast. It works great because it doesn't peel off like white tape, and it is also skin-colored. The sound produced when using Elasto-Plast is almost the same as your fingers. I highly recommend this product for your plucking hand—I use it when I feel a blister forming. To apply, peel off a length of about three inches, and place it on the finger with the overlap facing away from the part of the finger that addresses the string. The length of the tape should only be enough so that it overlaps only 1/4 to 1/2 inch. Also, one layer is all you want on the finger. It is very flexible and stays in place. Keep Elasto-Plast and Joha string oil in your bass case at all times. You do not want to try to play with a blister on your plucking hand that breaks open and bleeds.

When I first started playing upright, I mistakenly put on a heavy-gauge set of strings with high action and then took a week-long, five-hour-a-day strolling acoustic gig with a band playing at a fair. The first two fingers of my plucking had were bleeding by the end of the first day—forcing me to play with my middle and ring fingers!

The first finger and pinky of my fretting hand were also blistered.

Playing the upright doesn't have to be painful, and I don't want to scare any players away from the instrument, but there are rules to follow that will make it much easier. They include light-gauge strings, low action, Joha string oil, and Elasto-Plast. Playing the upright with a consistent schedule, at least one or two gigs a week, will help keep your calluses in shape. Pacing yourself, if you know you have three more sets to go, will also help. Don't play as hard as you can all the time—turn up your amp instead, and lighten up slightly on your attack, without sacrificing your tone.

- Joha string oil is available from Vitali Import 1-800-325-8154.
- Lemur Music carries a complete line of bass strings and accessories 1-800-246-BASS.
- Elasto-Plast is available at surgical supply stores or pharmacies.

Artist's Spotlight
E d g a r   W i l l i s

When it comes to blues/soul upright bass playing, the absolute master was the late Edgar Willis. His amazing gut-string tone and melodic phrasing graced the early recordings of Ray Charles. Oftentimes unconventional in his approach, he always made his melodic phrases fit the music with outstanding results.

Upper-register runs with a sweet, woody tone were Willis's hallmark, yet he never gave the impression of playing too busy. For example, check out the amazing "soulfulness" he brings to Ray Charles's "Georgia on My Mind"—this is the quintessential "uptown" blues ballad. His use of triplet patterns, swing, and dancing runs provided the musical backdrop for Ray's vocal interpretations. One might think that a bass player with a lot of facility might be "edgy" in his time feel, but Edgar played with one of the most relaxed and widest grooves imaginable.

Edgar was also a pioneer in the blues/funk field, and Charles's "Unchain My Heart," and "One Mint Julep" are perfect examples of his "funkiness." Other examples of his artistry include "Crying Time," "That Lucky Old Sun," "You Don't Know Me," and the great "Born to Lose"—all by Ray Charles (recordings circa 1960-70).

The tone of Edgar's bass is attributed to an upright bass played with gut strings—the perfect combination for expressing the music of Ray Charles.

When talking with players of that period, I was told that it was hard to hear Edgar because he didn't use an amp! Even in big concerts, the only device he used was a mike placed in front of his bass. Imagine playing in a concert hall with a full horn section and having to play as hard as you can—only being able to feel your bass sound!

Along with being a great blues bassist, Edgar could also make every song he played really swing. Purchase Ray Charles's Greatest Hits, Vol. 1, to hear what I'm talking about. I am very pleased to present these bass lines in the style of legendary bassist Edgar Willis.

In the style of EDGAR WILLIS

Recording

Start with a great-sounding bass, well set-up and intonated with the action high enough so that the strings don't buzz when played hard. Depending on the style of blues being recorded, use the appropriate string type (flatwound, roundwound, nylon tape flatwound).

THE ELECTRIC BASS

In the recording world, one company has had the most success: Fender. Precision and Jazz Basses are industry standards, and I recommend that you own one because it will work for you in any session. If you want a different type of sound, there are other basses that can be good alternatives. Below are some electric basses used in professional studios:

- The *Gibson Les Paul Signature* bass is a good, fat-sounding full-scale bass.
- *Hofner* basses have a unique sound that merges the electric bass with a hollowbody.
- *Kay* hollowbody electric basses are popular and sound great with flatwounds on them.
- *Washburn* acoustic bass guitars sound good, especially with flatwounds.

Direct Boxes

Going direct using a good tube direct box is one way of recording the straight signal from the bass. Although limited tone-wise, this is the preferred technique for most sessions. Below are some DI units used in professional studios:

- *Demeter* tube DI
- *Tube Works* tube DI
- *Manley* tube DI
- *Countryman* solid-state DI
- *Sescom* solid-state DI

Bass Pre-Amps

I also like to use a bass pre-amp with an XLR direct out or a 1/4 inch output plugged into the recording console. This allows me to get an amp-like tone that can cut through and be heard better in the track. Below are some units that are in use in professional studios:

- *Demeter* tube bass pre-amp
- *Alembic* F2B and F1X tube bass pre-amps
- *Glockenklang Bass Art* pre-amp (has a great adjustable distortion feature)
- *Aguilar* tube bass pre-amp

Amps

The most popular bass amp for recording is the 1960s Ampeg B15N Porta-Flex tube bass amp. Running a close second is the 1960s Fender "Blackface" Bassman tube bass amp (head). The Fender Bassman 100 (100 watts), Bassman 135 (135 watts), and Dual Showman are all excellent bass amps, too.

James Jamerson, of Motown fame, used the B15N exclusively, as did many other bassists, including Duck Dunn. The sound of the B15N is very deep and rich, with not much high end in the tone.

The ultimate blues bass rig would have to be a Fender Precision Bass with La Bella flatwound strings, plugged into an Ampeg B15N with the bass control on the amp turned wide open, and the treble control set at the midway point. The Ampeg B12 and B18 bass amps both sound great too, but the B15N is the industry standard. The B15N is a 35-watt amp, so take that into consideration—it might not be loud enough by itself. Glenn Worf, of The Bluebloods, in Nashville, uses two Ampeg amps plugged in together for his upright bass with an Underwood pickup. Ampeg has just reissued the B15N and has increased the output from the original 35 watts to 100 watts.

Miking Your Amp

When miking an amp, be sure that the microphone is placed as close to the speaker cone as possible. This keeps the delay between the DI and the amp track to a minimum. The DI track is recorded instantaneously, whereas the mike/amp track has a short delay caused by the time it takes for the sound of the speaker to reach the mike. If your recorded bass track is played a little on top of the beat or rushed, the mike track can be favored when mixing the tracks, making the track appear more relaxed. Another trick is to place the mike six to twelve inches away from the speaker, creating even more delay—this, when combined with the DI, can make the notes seem to sustain more and make the bass track sound very "wide."

The Fender "Blackface" Bassman tube head was used exclusively by legendary producer Rick Hall in Muscle Shoals, Alabama. His technique was to record a P-Bass with flatwounds into the Bassman, connected to a Fender cabinet with 12-inch speakers. The amp was then miked six to twelve inches away using an old tube microphone, yielding an incredibly deep, rich bass tone. A DI track was never used on the great tracks recorded by Rick, which include classics by Aretha Franklin. The mike track alone, along with the request by Rick for the bassist to play the bass as hard as possible, provided the amazing tone.

The Beatles also used a Bassman for recording.

TIP

Always set the bass cabinet directly on the floor. Do not play your amp when it is resting on wheels or on a chair; this decreases the low-end response considerably, and the tone is adversely affected.

For years, I installed permanent casters on my cabinets and never set them directly on the floor. I was playing at a club one night, and a bass player walked in and asked me why I didn't set my cabinet directly on the floor. He told me that it would sound much better if I did. So the next week, at that same club, I turned my cabinet over on its side, directly coupling with the floor and stage. The guys in the band came up to me later and said that my bass sounded incredible—what did I do? I instantly heard the difference, too, and I put removable casters on all of my cabinets. I would like to thank bassist Mike Berry, of the Bernie Pearl Blues Band for the tip.

THE UPRIGHT BASS

Carved basses are the best and offer a more "complex" tone than laminated or plywood instruments. However, laminated basses like Kay basses are widely used and can sound great when properly set up.

Miking

Recording an upright can be hard to do if proper mike technique isn't used. If possible, try a few different mikes, zeroing in on the mike that sounds best for your particular bass. Place the mike in front of the bass bridge, about five or six inches away, with the mike favoring the E-string slightly. (The E-string on most basses is the weakest in volume; favoring it will help create a better balance between the strings.) Experiment with different mike placements, but keep in mind the following: the sound of an upright bass develops a distance away from the instrument. Placing the mike a half an inch in front of the bridge will yield a less full-sounding track.

Pickups

Record a track with a pickup on your upright, too. The sound of a pickup, although trebly sometimes, can be blended in, adding to the character of the mike track. Record the mike and the pickup on separate tracks at the same time; this will allow the engineer to blend them together for the best sound in the final mix.

Underwood pickups are very popular, as are Barcus-Berry, Fishman, and David Gage. All of these units are piezo-based designs and will work for steel or gut strings. A good addition to any of these pickups is the Fishman Model-B bass pre-amp. It allows you to adjust the tone of the pickup if needed.

For greater volume when using steel strings, I recommend Pierre Joseph's "String-Charger" magnetic pickup (not for use with gut strings). It has a built-in jack for your piezo unit for blending with the magnetic pickup. You can play at a much higher volume before feedback with this set-up. For the ultimate in tone, I also recommend Schertler's "KP-Model" bridge pickup. Although expensive, it sounds very close to the actual sound of your bass. I use the KP on my bass, along with a Pierre Joseph String-Charger magnetic, and it sounds great.

Schertler: Via Furnasse, 6853 Ligornetto, Switzerland

Pierre Joseph's: 125 Locust St., Larkspur, CA 94939

Barcus-Berry: c/o BBE Sound Inc., 5381 Production Dr., Huntington Beach, CA 92649

Underwood and Fishman are available at Lemur Music 1-800-246-BASS.

TRACKING

When tracking bass, the rule is the same for both upright and electric: the tone comes from your hands. Don't depend on EQs, compressors, or engineers to fix any problems with your technique or sound. Recording requires good timing, a consistent level, and a solid tone from the bassist. If you have any problems with these requirements, you will find out on the first playback.

TECHNIQUE

A good way to prepare yourself for recording is to become comfortable playing through headphones and to record yourself with a home studio recorder, or even a small tape recorder taken to your gigs.

Recording yourself at all times will allow you to listen to your playing and edit out the problems in your style. Are you aware of the length and tone of every note? Are you rushing, dragging, or playing too far ahead or behind the beat? Are you playing right with the kick drum and being supportive to the vocalist or soloist? Are you playing too much or the wrong notes?

Paying attention to your playing at all times may seem detrimental to your music at first, but with time, your level of musicianship will rise far above that of bassists who don't care about how well they are playing or sounding. This type of approach is the common thread that all great bassists share. Get some headphones and a metronome, and start "shedding" your chops; your favorite bassist does, too. This preparation will allow you to create more easily in the studio.

PLUCKING THE STRINGS

Whether recording or playing live, a strong attack of each note is required. Concentrate on playing each note with a good, even stroke—one that will provide a nice, round tone. With the first and second fingers of your plucking hand, play slowly, alternating each finger until you find a stroke that sounds thick and strong. Play with the pads of your fingers, not the tips. I wouldn't recommend playing too closely to the bridge, as this yields a thinner tone. I like the sound of the fingers over the bass pickup or between the pickup and the end of the neck.

For the upright, play each note with a strong attack, too, favoring the pad and the side of the plucking fingers. Overall, play with a firm approach, learning to use dynamics without playing too softly, because a strong, round tone is required from the bass in most situations. It is better to play strongly, hitting a wrong note occasionally, than it is to play the correct notes tentatively or weakly—remember that!

Artist's Spotlight
Donald "Duck" Dunn

Donald "Duck" Dunn was one of the most respected electric bassists of our time. His work with the Stax Records house band (Booker T. and the MG's) created and defined the "Memphis Sound." His teaming with legendary drummer (the late) Al Jackson Jr., created a "primer" for rhythm sections that is studied to this day.

What made Duck's bass playing so influential? His strong note choices, tone, and "in-the-pocket" grooves, which have been the backbone that many artists have depended on for thirty-plus years. His credits include Eric Clapton, Otis Redding, Wilson Pickett, Sam & Dave, Albert King, George Harrison, John Fogerty, and many others.

Heavily influenced by blues and country, Duck blended those styles and formed the blues/soul approach that made him famous. A big part of his sound is attributed to his strong, driving attack—along with his uncluttered, creative bass lines. Duck has used a 1958 Fender Precision Bass for most of his career, along with an Ampeg B15N for most of the Stax recordings. He later used an Ampeg SVT for his concert and studio work. Duck normally used flat-wounds, but he also occasionally used roundwounds on his reissue P-Bass with a Jazz Bass neck on it.

Concerning the blues, Duck's lines were so appropriate and fitting, I feel it is important to study his style. Always right on and in the groove, his lines are "textbook" blues. One of his strengths was that he always let you know what chord is being played by playing a strong downbeat, while also playing the best lines in the traditional sense for the song. He defined bass playing by playing lines fitting the bass with a strong, rhythmic groove—Duck Dunn was a true classic.

In the style of "DUCK" DUNN

Setting Up Your Electric Bass

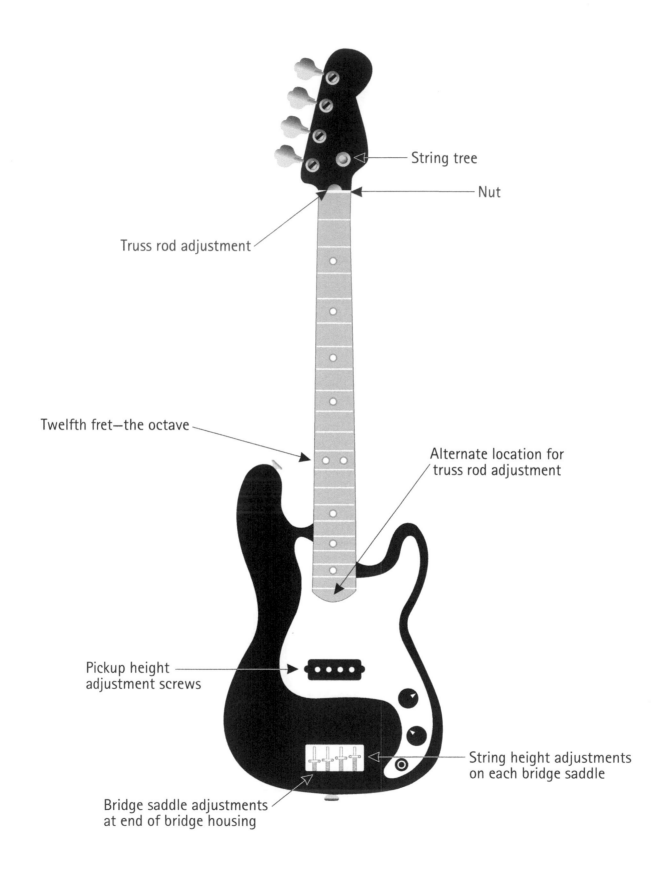

String tree

Nut

Truss rod adjustment

Twelfth fret—the octave

Alternate location for truss rod adjustment

Pickup height adjustment screws

String height adjustments on each bridge saddle

Bridge saddle adjustments at end of bridge housing

Truss Rod Adjustment

Install new strings, tune the bass to pitch, and set the truss rod. View the neck in a well-lit area from the end of the peghead, looking down the front of the neck, checking the G-side and the E-side for bow.

The neck should have a little bit of "relief" or *forward bow*. ("Forward bow" means that the peghead should bow away from you when the bass is in playing position.) Back bow will make all of the notes buzz. Not enough forward bow will make the notes from the fifth fret to the nut on all the strings buzz when played hard.

TIP

The truss rod should only be turned a quarter of a turn each time, and the bass should be retuned after each adjustment. You do not want to force a turn—it will most certainly break. Clockwise tightens or straightens the neck. Be gentle. Some basses require taking the neck off when adjusting the truss rod.

String Height

Next, set the action or string height of each string at the bridge. Retune after each adjustment. The G and D string height will probably be set slightly lower than the E and A strings. You should be able to play your bass acoustically (in a small room like a bathroom) with no buzzes or noises when you play hard.

Most pro bassists keep their action set medium-high for clarity without buzzes. Don't set your action too high—find the "sweet spot" that allows for ease of playing with no buzzes and a good tone.

Nut Action

The nut action should be set next. Take your bass to a repairperson for this adjustment, unless you are capable and have the necessary nut files. When the action at the nut is too high, the notes in the lower register can play sharp.

Set the nut action so that it is as low as it can be without the open strings buzzing when played hard. This "frees up" the left hand for easier lower register playing and the bass will play more in tune over the whole neck.

TIP

If you have more than a business card's thickness between the first fret and the underside of the string, then your nut action needs to be lowered. If your open strings rattle at the nut, you need to put a shim under the nut because it is set too low.

Intonation

Finally, intonate each string by playing each open string or twelfth fret harmonic and getting it in tune with your tuner. Then play the twelfth fret of the string you just tuned, and see how in tune it is with the open string or harmonic. If it's flat, move the bridge saddle toward the twelfth fret a little bit, and then retune the open string.

Repeat until the twelfth fret and the open string are reading the same on your tuner. If the twelfth fret is sharp, move the bridge saddle away from the twelfth fret, and then retune the open string and check it again against the twelfth fret.

Pickup Height

The last adjustment should be the pickup height in relation to the strings. Set the pickup height so that the balance from string to string is even. Sometimes, the E-string side of the pickup will need to be set lower than the G-string side in order to have a good balance.

Set the height so that you are comfortable and not hampered by the pickup position. Don't set the pickup any closer than 1/4 of an inch to the string—the magnetism could lessen the sustain. 1/4 to 3/8 inch clearance between the string and the pickup is usually adequate. You may need to be add foam under the pickups in order to adjust them to your preferred height.

When in doubt, take your bass to a qualified repairperson for adjustment. Watch and learn so you can do your own set-ups.

Artist's Spotlight
Tommy Shannon

A Texas-based blues bassist, Tommy Shannon provided the solid contemporary bass lines for the late Stevie Ray Vaughan. Tommy has been a respected player in the Texas blues scene for many years, particularly in Austin, the home base for many blues and rock artists. Tommy's career started off "with a bang" when he played on Johnny Winter's first album, *Johnny Winter*, which was a huge success, making him an in-demand bassist. When Tommy hooked up with Stevie Ray and drummer Chris Layton, forming the band Double Trouble, he found the perfect vehicle for his rock-solid blues/rock bass style.

Tommy has always impressed me with his in-the-pocket, note-perfect grooving style. He never tries to call attention to himself, which to me displays self-confidence and a giving attitude—the perfect attributes for any bassist striving to become a great player. When describing his style, I always gravitate towards one word: solid. The most popular bassists have this quality, along with the ability to create within the role of the bass.

When Tommy plays blues bass, he shows a keen knowledge of the blues tradition, playing classic, "on-the-money" bass lines.

Tone-wise, I was blown away the first time I heard a Stevie Ray Vaughan CD. Tommy's recorded bass sound is round, warm, and thick—really filling out the bottom of the band. He has relied on a '62 Jazz Bass for most of his recording, along with a miked amp. After Stevie's fatal helicopter crash, Tommy found success again with the critically acclaimed Arc Angels, an Austin-based band that included Charlie Sexton and Double Trouble bandmate Chris Layton. Tommy's bass work on all of Stevie Ray's albums is as good as it gets, and I recommend that you pick them up and study his style.

In the style of TOMMY SHANNON

Electric or Upright?

Electric or upright bass? This is a dilemma faced by many bassists, especially young players. But consider this: if you played two instruments, wouldn't you be able to work more and be more valuable to the producers and artists that you work for?

I decided to start playing the upright when I was thirty years old, and it has been a blessing to my music and career. It has made it possible for me to work more consistently, and the effect on my electric playing has also been very positive. The increased hand strength, directly related to my upright playing, has improved my dexterity and control on the electric, while giving me a "firmer" sound and attack.

Besides that, I have a blast playing the upright; the musical expression it affords is boundless. I like the fact that I can really "lay into the string" and play as hard as I want, creating different tonal textures. The first year of playing upright was hard (intonation, physicality, mental adjustment), but after that initial year, I was finally able to start playing the instrument—instead of it playing me.

Set-Up

Here are some tips on getting started with the upright bass:

- Buy the best bass that you can afford. Again, carved basses are the best, but they're also more expensive. Laminated or plywood basses like Kay basses are widely used and can sound great when properly set up.

- When purchasing an upright bass, be sure it has no cracks in the top, a bent bridge, or deep grooves in the fingerboard. If a bass has some of these problems, take them into consideration when purchasing. Do you know a qualified repairperson? Is it cheaper to buy a new instrument already in good condition?

- Install adjustment wheels into the existing bridge—*this is important.* Sometimes, depending on the weather, I have to raise or lower my bridge frequently as the seasons change. The temperature and humidity strongly affect the string height of most basses.

- Have the fingerboard planed and leveled on worn basses. If the fingerboard is uneven, the notes will buzz, and it will be hard to play in tune.

- Install a set of light- or medium-gauge steel strings. Start off with a set of Thomastik Spiro-Core weich-gauge steel strings, Pirastro "Jazzer" steel strings, or Jargar medium-gauge steel strings. (When a gut-sounding steel string is preferred, use Jargar.) For gut strings, use the La Bella #980 Pro Set.

- WARNING: Do not take off all the strings at once. Change one string at a time, leaving tension on the other strings. If there is no tension on the top of the bass from the strings, the soundpost will fall over!

- It is very important to have the soundpost adjusted. The soundpost is a round, tube-like, wooden post inside the bass that connects the inside of the top of the bass with the inside of the back. This post transfers vibrations from the top to the back, producing the sound that comes out of the f-holes. A qualified repairperson can move this post and adjust the tonal response of the instrument. Never put string tension on a bass with no soundpost—it will crack the top!

- Have the nut action adjusted. This very important adjustment will allow easier playing with the left hand. The distance between the bottom of the string and the fingerboard, right in front of the nut, should be about the thickness of a business card. This will free up the left hand and lessen fatigue.

Do not try the above adjustments yourself. Take your bass to a qualified orchestral instrument repairperson. Call your local high school or orchestral dealer for a referral.

Practice Tips

- When standing with the instrument, set the bottom peg height so that your nose is even with the low G note on the E-string.

- Right-handed players should keep their inside leg (left leg) behind the bass, with the inside of the left knee touching the back of the instrument. This will, with time, make playing much easier on the left hand because of the proper wrist angle this stance affords. Standing with your left leg beside the bass instead of behind it will make it harder to play and will detract from the strength of the left hand—a straight wrist is best. (Left-handed players should apply the above recommendations to the right leg.)

- Stand with your weight balanced on both of your feet.

- Pluck the strings with your plucking fingers pointing downward. This will allow you to use both the side and the pad of your finger. This combination produces a bigger sound, as opposed to playing with the tips of the fingers only, which is considerably weaker sounding.

- Pluck each note firmly. Place your plucking hand above the fingerboard—a couple of inches from the end of the fingerboard. This position will produce a clear tone with good volume. Placing the plucking hand higher up the neck towards the nut produces a softer tone. Keep your fretting hand elbow raised slightly when playing. This allows for better intonation and accuracy. Play major scales up and down the neck and across the strings, listening for intonation.

- Be patient. With time, you will be having fun and expanding your potential as a professional bassist. You will get past the physical adjustment if you maintain a consistent playing schedule. If you only play once a week, you probably won't make much progress, so try to play your upright as much as possible.

Artist's Spotlight

Keith Ferguson

The late Keith Ferguson was one of the best blues-based bassists to ever come out of Texas. A personal favorite of Muddy Waters, he was a dominant force in the Austin blues scene, and his impact helped define what is now considered Texas-style blues.

Keith was a founding member of the Fabulous Thunderbirds and played on their groundbreaking recordings from 1974 to 1983. In addition to his work with the T-Birds and Muddy Waters, he also played with Albert Collins, Johnny Winter, and the great Cajun/blues band the Tailgators, whom I had the pleasure of seeing many times.

Keith's bass style was very slippery, with a lot of movement—at the same time, his lines were never too busy. They were always within the traditional blues style, yet he put his own unique groove and twist on them. With his right-handed vintage P-Bass played upside down (he was a lefty), Keith could also play one of the "nastiest" grooves I have ever heard. His tone was downright "gnarly," but he also got a deep, round sound that really made people want to dance. He played aggressively, producing a strong note with a punchy sound.

Keith's recorded work with the T-Birds is the epitome of Texas blues bass, and that, along with the album *Swamp Rock* by the Tailgators, showcases his very unique style. I'm proud to present these lines in the style of Keith Ferguson.

Modern Blues

In the style of KEITH FERGUSON

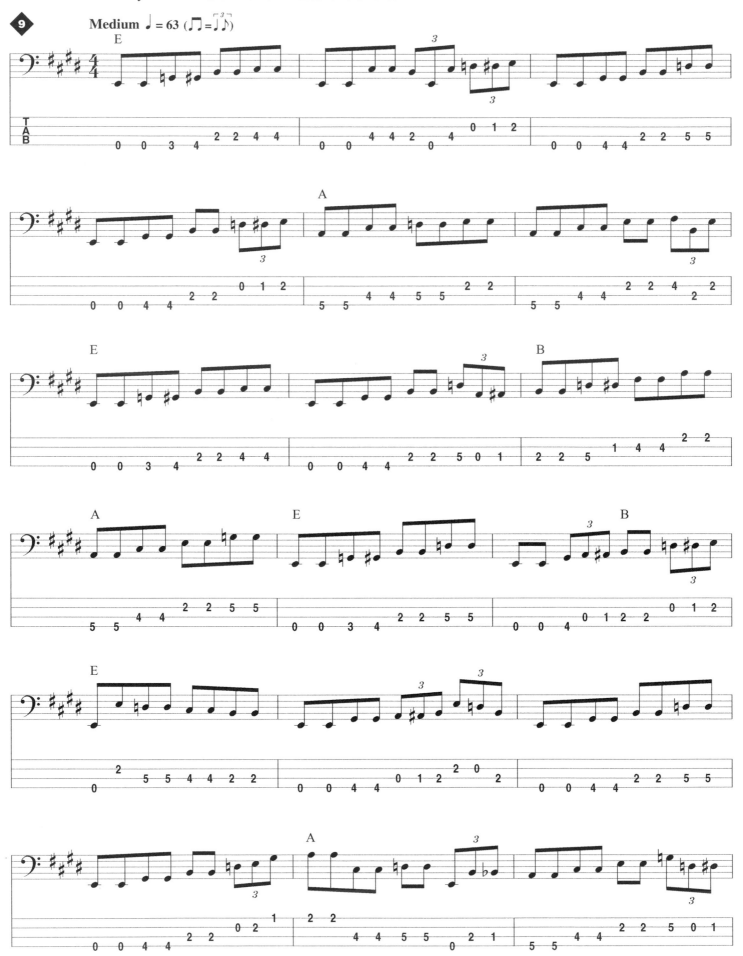

The Blues Tradition

Throughout the years, the role of the blues bassist has evolved, blending together many regional styles and necessitating adjustments on the part of today's bassists. These adjustments must be made in knowledge, repertoire, and particularly in the area of recording.

Today's records don't sound like the old records, and they never will. Part of the beauty of old blues recordings is the sound and the "vibe." The artfulness can be duplicated by players of today, but the archaic technology of that time cannot. The blues artists on the old records were not the only creative forces of our time, but they were the pioneers, and that "newness" of the artform cannot be duplicated.

Today's blues bassists, however, have the opportunity to push the envelope of the blues, with tradition as their foundation. A bassist with knowledge of both traditional blues *and* modern styles is a force to be reckoned with. "Knowing the book" and playing the right bass lines at a blues gig is an absolute necessity—your lines propel the soloists and help create the foundation for the groove.

When I first started playing on blues gigs, I played too much, thinking that I had to play intricate, technical bass lines. The fact is, blues is about the feel and the interplay of the players in the band. You have nothing to prove on a blues gig. The need for solid, grooving bass playing has never been stronger.

A common mistake is to overplay, forgetting that "meat-and-potatoes" bass playing is what's needed: big fat tone, killer groove and feel, dynamics, subtlety, and finesse. You are not the star of the band; you are the *soul* of the band. Remember that.

Be a smart player, playing consistent patterns that make sense and fit the song and feel. When you choose a pattern, *stick with it.* It isn't wise to change bass patterns in most blues songs—consistency is best. Listen to the other players, and meld with their style, while at the same time putting down some serious supportive lines and grooves.

More Blues Bass Lines
Slow Swing
à la EDGAR WILLIS

Up-Tempo Blues

à la JERRY JEMMOTT

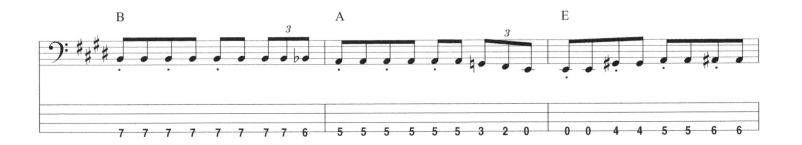

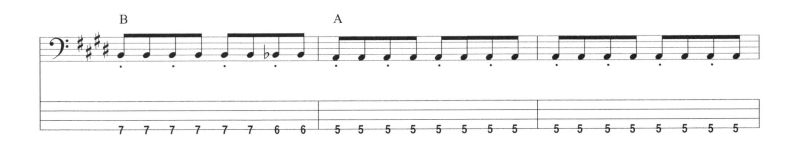

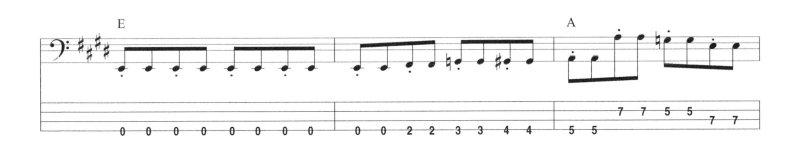

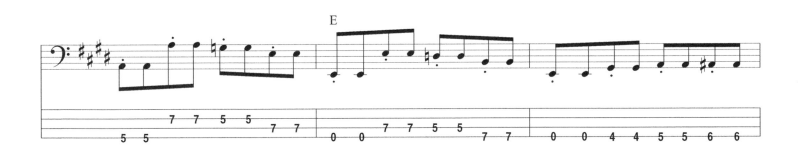

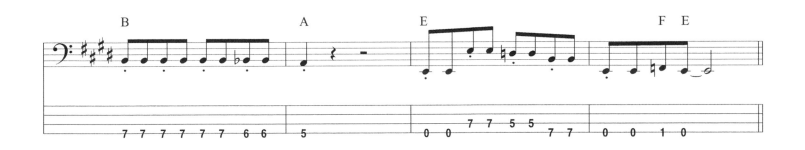

Slow Blues

Medium Blues

à la LARRY TAYLOR

More Blues Bass Lines
"Two" Feel
à la WILLIE DIXON

Funky Blues

à la B.B. KING

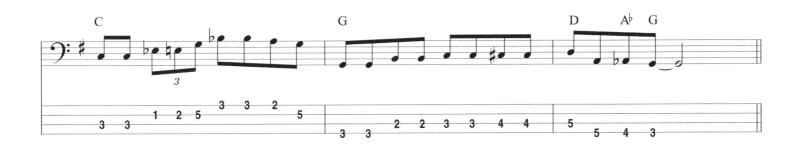

More Blues Bass Lines
"Two" Feel
à la LARRY TAYLOR

Medium Blues

Slow Blues

Minor Blues

Blues in F

More Blues Bass Lines

Bouncy Blues

Lazy Blues

A Note from the Author

Within these pages, I have tried to offer fellow bass players a good source for learning how to play authentic "real" blues bass lines; it was my goal that even the most learned blues bassist have fun with this book. Hopefully, you have gotten as much enjoyment from reading this book as I have from writing it. Listening to classic recordings and offering bass lines in the style of the great blues bassists featured in this book has been a great, humbling experience. It has given me an opportunity to strengthen my own blues playing as well.

Besides learning the bass lines in this book, go and hang out at your local blues clubs and "sit in." It's important that you meet and play with other blues players—the final step towards becoming a successful blues bassist. Lastly, groove every note, and play from the heart.

Good luck,

Keith Rosiér

Keith Rosiér

About the Author

KEITH ROSIÉR has played bass professionally for twenty-five years. An electric and upright bassist, he has worked with Joe Houston, Big Jay McNeely, Steve Earle, Jann Browne, Charlie Sexton, Alexander, and others. As a session player, his film credits include *Beverly Hills Cop II*, *California*, *Exposed*, *Blue Rodeo*, *Return to Two-Moon Junction*, and *The Effects of Magic*. Keith lives with his wife Denise, and their daughter, Madeleine, in the Los Angeles area.

Other books by Keith Rosiér:
The Lost Art of Country Bass

The Credits

Keith would like to thank:

Baby Madeleine, Denise, Mom, Doug Johnson, Jeff Schroedl, Doug Downing, Dan Hughart, Kinko's, Alexander, Michael Jay, Richard Cocco Jr. and La Bella, John Carruthers, Glockenklang, Toni Buffa and Lemur Music, Richard Johnston, and Harry.

Original Concept Design: Doug Johnson
Original TAB and Music Engraving: Dan Hughart
Special thanks to all at Hal Leonard Corporation.

SESSION PERSONNEL

Larry Mitchell: Drums

Alexander: Electric guitars

Larry David: Piano, organ, and harmonica

Keith Rosiér: Upright and electric bass

Ian Miller: Recording/mixing/mastering engineer

Matt Barnes: Additional recording

Produced by Keith Rosiér for Madeleine Productions.

Jump 'n' Blues T-Shirt

Price: $17.00 each; Shipping is $3.00.

Please send check or money order (U.S. funds only) payable to:

> Keith Rosiér
> P.O. Box 50732
> Irvine, CA 92619-0732

Please specify L, XL, or XXL. Large will be sent if no size is specified.

Available in black only.

Please include mailing address.

If you would like to correspond with Keith, send a self-addressed, stamped envelope to the above address.